VENTRILOQUISM

The Best Book in Print on Ventriloquism

Liz LaMac and Little Joe

VENTRILOQUISM

For Health, Wealth, and Happiness

By

Liz LaMac

Copyright 2014

Published
By
Generation Publishers
Spencer, West Virginia

DEDICATED TO

My husband Mack Boggs, a "one in a million catch" and a true partner for life.

And

My five wonderful children: Penny, Sheree, Jeff, Sonia, and Martin and all of their families—whose love and encouragement keeps me creative and in tune with the world.

And To My Readers:
The outgoing, fun-loving and creative minds: May you spread your love and happiness to the four corners of the earth, via the Ventriloquial process.

ACKNOWLEDGEMENTS

To the many Authors who have written books and articles on the Healing Power of Laughter.

To my many Ventriloquial friends for their help and encouragement.

Special thanks to Bill Boley, who has always been willing to share his ideas with other Ventriloquists.

To Alan Semok, for creating Little King Joe exactly the way I wanted him.

To Paul Winchell for writing *Ventriloquism for Fun and Profit*, the book that taught me to Ventriloquise.

To Jimmy Nelson and his dummy, Danny O'Day, for their interest, encouragement and friendship, and for teaching me to think one sound while actually saying another. And for helping me acquire the distance voice.

To Walter Cardwell, my Fan Club President and Photographer; for his friendship, and for thousands of pictures.

Foreword

In reading over the "galleys" before this book went to print, I was impressed by the sincerity of the author. Liz LaMac has a disarming style. Yes, she is "teaching" the art of ventriloquism, but she is also "informing" us about ventriloquism, keeping the reader interested while learning, something I have missed while reading other "how to" books.

Having been a professional ventriloquist myself since the 1950s, and an amateur performer many years prior to that, I only wish a volume such as this had been available to me when I was starting out. It would have made the learning process a lot easier for me.

I am particularly pleased that Liz teaches us to "think one sound while actually saying another," a process I have advocated for many years. And I am pleased that she learned the method from me. Try it. It really works!

A lot of things "work" in this book, and I believe you will find it much easier to become an accomplished ventriloquist than you might have thought, thanks to the Liz LaMac method of teaching the art. Her emphasis on laughter and good, wholesome material is refreshing and laudable.

Ventriloquism has been with us for centuries, and will be around for centuries to come. It has been a lot of fun for me and I know it will be a lot of fun for you. There's nothing more gratifying than hearing the laughter of your audience. And, as Liz says, laughter is, after all, the best medicine.

Jimmy Nelson

TABLE OF CONTENTS

Chapter 3
IMPROVING THE VOICE

Chapter 4
STRENGTHENING THE TONGUE MUSCLES

Chapter 5
FIRST STEPS TO VENTRILOQUIZING

PART TWO: The basic techniques for acquiring your ventrilocution and building your partner's personality and style.

Chapter 6
YOUR VENTRILOCUTION

Chapter 7
WHEN THE DUMMY TALKS

Chapter 8
THE MOMENT YOU'VE BEEN AWAITING

Chapter 9
BREATHING LIFE INTO THE DUMMY

Chapter 10
SPEAKING FOR TWO

PART THREE: Going one step further with your ventrilocution. And how and where to use the art of ventriloquism for health, wealth and happiness.

"...the old man laughed loud and joyously, shook up the details of his anatomy from head to foot, and ended by saying that such a laugh was money in a man's pocket, because it cut down the doctor's bills like everything."

MARK TWAIN in *TOM SAWYER*

Chapter 1

THE HEALING POWER OF LAUGHTER

So You Want to Be a Ventriloquist

Before we start learning to become a ventriloquist please turn to the back of the book and read the glossary. If you are going to be a ventriloquist, than you need to know and use the proper terms.

Now, we are ready. Did you know that being a ventriloquist will make you laugh? Just seeing a dummy sitting on your knee will bring a smile to your face. You will be fascinated with him. And while you are trying to think of funny things for the little tyke to say, your mind can not be on troublesome subjects. You can only think about one thing at a time. So when the dummy says funny things, it will make you laugh; when you laugh others will laugh with you. Did you know laughter is like a medicine; a medicine that is healing to the mind, body, and soul.

Doctors have recognized the healing value of laughter for many centuries. Of course ventriloquism, as most of us see it, is most often used for the amusement and entertainment it offers to the entertainer, and to the audience. But, the use of ventriloquism has spread out from the entertainment field, and spilled over into the schools and churches. It is now being used as a teaching aid.

Although ventriloquism is a remarkable teaching aid, I believe the most important attribute of ventriloquy lies in the field of therapy for the sick, depressed, and

11

mentally ill. The very fact that a ventriloquist can cause others to laugh, makes it an avenue for the healing process. Just listen to what the physician, James J. Walsh, wrote in his book, *Laughter and Health*.

While laughter is a mystery from its mental aspect, it is easy to appreciate its far-reaching physical effects. The diaphragm, the principal organ involved in it, is in intimate anatomical relations with all the organs in the body that carry on the physical life. Whenever there are convulsive movements in the diaphragm, they are sure to be affected by them. As laughter always makes us feel better for having indulged in it, it is evident that the effect of the movements of the diaphragm and the large organs in its neighborhood is beneficial.

Besides, the mental effect brushes away the dreads and fears that constitute the basis of so many diseases or complaints and lifts men out of the slough of despondence into which they are so likely to fall when they take themselves over seriously.

Therapy Through a Dummy

Volumes could be written concerning therapy through a dummy or a puppet. And there have been many books and many, many articles written about astounding breakthroughs in serious, therapeutic communication, including laughter. Different ways of reaching the distressed and disturbed are being discovered daily, by using puppets, dummies, and humor.

Many therapists, especially those in hospital settings, are taking advantage of this ancient art of ventriloquy and its seemingly healing values, not only to those people observing, but to the ventriloquist as well. I know that when I am depressed or ill, I can get one of my dummies and just start talking to it like a friend. The first thing I know, I am laughing, and the dummy is kidding around, and I'm feeling better. I sometimes believe that when I am sad my dummy looks sad because I am not putting enough into his actions. When I see him looking sad, I try to cheer him up, thereby cheering myself up as well. It's like the great philosopher Carruth said, "Each to each the looking glass reflects the other that doeth pass."

In the summer of 1978, I went on a tour of mental and veteran hospitals. This was one of the most rewarding times I have experienced in my life. I would perform on the stage for those who were able to come to the auditorium. Then, I would set my dummy and puppets on a hospital cart, and along with the doctors, nurses, and therapists, go to the wards to visit on a one-to-one basis with those patients who were too ill to come to the stage show.

Sometimes we worked until the wee hours of the morning. The hospital personnel were always amazed at the results the dummy received, and would almost always plead with us to see one more patient. There was no way we could say no.

I cannot describe the feelings I had one might when talking to a man covered up by a blanket at a veteran's hospital. I thought the man looked very small, but asked no questions. At first, my dummy couldn't seem

13

to get through to him. There was a crowd around the bed as the dummy tried to talk to him, but he did not respond. Then a smile started slowly and spread across his almost stone-like face. I looked up and tears were streaming down the faces of the other patients and the hospital attendants. What I hadn't realized was the man was without arms or legs. He had been injured in the war and had just recently been told that he now had cancer. It had been a long time since he had smiled. This was a very rewarding night for everyone involved.

But aside, from all the therapeutic and psychological benefits, ventriloquism is the great form of fun and laughter: it is pure enjoyment. There again, you can't separate the fun and laughter from the healing aspect; nor would you want to! Have we not heard all our lives, laughter is the best medicine?

Laughter: The Best Medicine

I once had an old book, printed before 1900, that told the story of a young woman who went to the doctor and told him she was sick all over. She felt so badly that she couldn't hold her head up at times. After a thorough examination the doctor found nothing physically wrong with her.

Puzzled, the doctor started asking her questions about her home life and soon found out that she was married to a drunkard, who would come home every night and beat her.

The wise doctor studied the case for a few minutes and then he said, "The only thing I can prescribe for you is a schedule of laughter. I want you to laugh when you wake up in the morning, laugh at 10:00 a.m., laugh at noon, and then laugh at 3:00 p.m. And laugh again at supper time. I want you to laugh when your husband comes home drunk. I want you to laugh again if he hits you." The lady agreed to try this unusual treatment.

She laughed at the allotted times during the day and when her husband came home drunk, she started laughing. It made him angry and he hit her even harder, but she kept on laughing. After a few days of this strange schedule she noticed a great change in her own behavior. She was getting her work done faster and a few times she even caught herself humming a little tune. She was definitely feeling better.

The drunkard noticed the change in his wife, and began to look forward to her laughter. Soon he was laughing with her. And, as the story went, the lady soon laughed herself well and her husband laughed himself sober.

Doctors and nurses all over the world are using laughter to keep up the morale of their patients and sometimes for a direct method of healing them.

On with the Laughter

Lawrence J. Peter, co-author of *The Laughter Prescription*, tells us: "I wouldn't recommend laughter as a cure-all for anything but the blues. Still, laughter does facilitate the healing process. It may even act as a preventive to illness. Since people with a depressed outlook are more vulnerable to certain diseases than people who have a sense of humor about life."

Even before 1600 an English person wrote in a textbook on psychiatry about the therapeutic value of humor. His name was Robert Burton and he said, "the wit makes the body young, lively, and fit for any manner of employment."

The Bible (Proverbs 17:22) says, "A merry heart doeth good, like a medicine; a broken spirit drieth the bones."

So you see, being a ventriloquist has many more rewards in store for you than you ever dreamed possible. The very first time you put that sock puppet on your hand, you'll see smiles on the faces of those around you. This will cause you to smile, and the smiles soon become contagious. So, hurry!

Chapter2

WHAT IS VENTRILOQUISM?

It Is an Illusion

What is ventriloquism? It is the art of speaking or producing more than one voice or sound, and making that voice or sound appear to come from an object or person other than the speaker. Ventriloquism is an illusion.

Just as in magic we don't actually see a woman cut in half, we know what we are seeing is just an illusion. The magician tells us what we are going to see. He suggests to our subconscious mind what we will see, and we are willing to go along with his suggestions. Because, he is a performer, and we know he has practiced long hours to entertain us, and we want to see what he suggests. This willingness on our part helps the magician to create the illusion.

In ventriloquism, the audience wants the dummy to talk, thus helping the ventriloquist create the illusion. The ventriloquist's voice never leaves his throat. He may imitate distant sounds, but the distant sound is still made in the voice box—so—now we know, we cannot really throw our voice. But remember, we can create that illusion. How is the illusion created? It's like playing a trick on someone. Only in this case, we play our trick on their ears, and use their eyes to affirm the trick. We don't really throw our voice, but it appears that we do; therefore, we often use the phrase, "throwing your voice."

17

Of all of our five senses, hearing is the least effective. How many times have you heard a sound and couldn't tell from what direction it came? The ventriloquist takes advantage of this confusion of hearing. He knows if his audience sees something move or fall, and at the same time hears a sound, they will naturally think the sound came from the object they saw move or fall.

If they see the dummy's mouth moving and hear a voice that is synchronized with its lip movement, they assume the dummy is talking. Easy, right?

No, it is not so easy. Our lips have to be motionless to complete the illusion. We have to imitate a voice that will sound as if it is a few feet from us. Just seeing a dummy on a performer's knee suggests that he is going to talk. When the dummy's mouth moves and we hear a voice, and at the same time the performer's mouth isn't moving, we assume the dummy is doing the talking. The illusion is complete. The performer is ventriloquizing.

Is Ventriloquism for You?

Ventriloquism is for you if you want to have fun, "throwing your voice." If you want to be recognized as a celebrity or as an entertainer, or if you like to be the life of the party or the center of attention at social gatherings, then Ventriloquism is for you. If you have a burning desire to be on stage, to be recognized as a singer, or as a dancer—yes, ventriloquism can help you achieve those goals also.

But, if you are interested in just making others happy and seeing the smiles spread across their faces, ventriloquism is still for you.

Anyone with a normal voice box can learn ventriloquism. If you can talk, you can ventriloquize. One of my students had a blocked nasal passage, but it didn't stop him from learning to be a good ventriloquist. He picked out a Dummy character that sounded great with a nasal twang.

What's the Age Limit?

Very funny, age limit: I hear these questions all the time about age:

* Am I too old to start to learn ventriloquism?
* Am I too young to have a dummy and start performing?
* At what age should a child start taking ventriloquial lessons?

It is just like picking a cane. My grandpappy told my daddy that the time to pick a cane is when you find the perfect branch or stick. "Pick it when you find it," he said.

Now, I'm telling you, the time and age to become a ventriloquist is whatever age you happen to be when you get the desire to be one. In other words, your age doesn't matter a hill of beans. If you are 4 to 104 you'll still make a good entertainer if you have that burning desire to be one.

Your First Partner

As you start to study ventriloquism, you will need a partner. This need not be the partner you are going to work with on stage. So don't rush out and buy a five hundred dollar dummy. All you need at this time is a hand puppet. You can buy one or make one. You will need this puppet from the very beginning to form the habit of synchronizing your ventriloquial voice with your hand movements. You can learn to do this with a hand puppet, and later the change to a ventriloquial dummy will be natural.

You can make a puppet to begin with out of a sock—a regular tube sock. (A tube sock is one that doesn't have a heel sewn or woven into it.) Put the sock on your hand, with about three to four inches of the toe extending over the fingers. Now take the toe part, and push it back into your fingers, forming a mouth. You may use small pins to hold the mouth in place, if you like. Also, you can use small rubber bands to make ears on your puppet. Now, you can add anything you want. But the three basic things your sock puppet needs are a mouth, eyes, and nose. Anything else is optional. You can add hair, hair ribbons, a beard, a tie, or whatever you want to put on your sock puppet.

One of the first things you need to know when you start to learn the art of ventriloquism is this: When you step on stage or sit down in front of your mirror to practice, "you become an actor." In a sense, you become two actors. You have to play the straight man's role and also portray the comedian through your dummy. You need to act so well that the audience will think there are actually two people talking. You will have to work overtime to perfect this illusion. You will be studying the parts for two people.

Not only will you need to learn the dummy's part, you will have to perfect its actions and create a voice for it that will sound as if it is coming from it. Call it "throwing your voice," if you like. This is the illusion you are trying to create. You want the voice to sound a short distance from your throat, as if it is coming straight from the dummy's mouth.

To better create this illusion, you must think of the dummy as a real person talking to you. After much practice the dummy will take on its own personality, and you will be able to think just as fast for him as you do for yourself. He will even surprise you with his witty remarks.

One word of caution: He is only real "on stage," which means when he is on your knee and you are performing or practicing. As soon as you step "off stage," he goes into the suitcase. He is no longer real—he is a dummy. For a grown-up to talk about a dummy as though he is a real person "off stage" is both childish and repulsive. You can refer to his personality, as you will not want to change it. We will discuss this in depth in a later lesson. All you need to remember for now is that when the show's over, the dummy goes into the case.

But you still need to enjoy the dummy and have fun with it. Just learn when to put him away. My dummy, King Joe, has a favorite jogging suit that he relaxes in before show time. Just having him sitting out before a show helps me get in the mood for performing. And then, changing him into his stage clothes prepares us both psychologically for the performance. You just don't want to go overboard.

But never pass up an opportunity to get free publicity shots. Once when I had a dentist appointment, I called ahead and got permission to bring "little Joe" for some unique photographs. It was also good public relations.

What Lies Ahead

I've been a performer and teacher of ventriloquism for many years. I have written several published children's books and, for many years, wrote a syndicated column for children. This accounts for my down-to-earth, simple way of writing and my ability to explain things on a level that all ages can understand. I am the first and, maybe, the only person who has taught ventriloquism at a college. My interest and activities in using ventriloquism for therapy have brought me great satisfaction. The lessons here are adapted from those I used in teaching both college and private students.

This course will help you to obtain the ventriloquial voice, adding depth and direction with each lesson. You will be able to analyze your voice for individual direction and style. You will read about stage techniques, and learn show biz tips that will allow you to master the secrets of the great ventriloquists. You will have the courage to write your own script and stage your own shows.

You will learn how ventriloquism will improve your speech. Most of all you will learn what makes people laugh, and you will learn to laugh with them. If you have perseverance and a burning desire to succeed, nothing can stop you, and no goal is too high to obtain. A whole new facet of living awaits you. You may throw your voice and land on stage.

Now, take your time and enjoy your lessons on ventriloquism, which are based on facts, tips, and experiences of famous ventriloquists through the ages.

CHAPTER 3

IMPROVING THE VOICE

Our Normal Voice

Before we are able to develop a ventriloquial voice, we must know something about how we produce our normal voice. This is not a simple procedure. We started producing sounds as soon as we were born and gradually produced different sounds until we were actually symbolizing. From the very first time we started producing sound, environment played a large part in the development of our voice. The background and environment of our parents, and those associated with us in the early years of our life, helped make our voice what it is today.

We might say that many of the characteristics of our voice were learned or imitated. If this is the case, we can unlearn the unattractive characteristics and imitate more pleasant sounds.

Our voice mechanisms and their locations also help decide, to a large degree, what we will sound like. Sometimes we do not use these organs to the best advantage or we learn incorrect habits at an early age.

To produce sound, we must have energy and vibration. The energy is produced by the air passing through the vocal cords. In order to form the sounds we desire and need, we must control the stream of air passing through the vocal cords. We are able to control this air stream with the use of the diaphragm.

The vocal cords (two bands of elastic-like tissue) are inside the larynx and when the vocal cords are close together, air rushing between them produces sounds. This is a reflex action. We don't think about pulling the vocal cords together so we can speak. We just open our mouths and the reflex action takes over.

However, this reflex action will not take over when you are trying to produce a ventriloquial voice. You will have to think what you want the vocal cords to do and how you want them stretched, because the shape and stretch in the cords determines the pitch (highness or lowness) of the voice. After you have formed the habit of speaking ventriloquially, it will become a reflex action. The more you practice, the sooner the reflex action will take over.

To simulate the action of the vocal cords, close your lips tightly and force air through them until you hear a sound.

Although the vocal cords are capable of producing a wide range of pitches and volume, something else is needed. When you play the guitar, you need nothing but energy and a vibration. But without the guitar box with the hole in it, the sounds might be weak and unpleasant. The hollow of the guitar serves as a resonance. Resonance amplifies the sound.

The vocal cord tone is subject to changes by resonance: that is, the amplifying or building up of parts of the tone. Normal voice sounds are resonated, to some extent, by the bones of the chest, head, larynx, and sinus cavities, but mostly by the three major cavities: the throat, nose, and mouth.

When moving from one empty house to another, you get a perfect example of the resonance and building up of tone. As you move the furniture out, you begin to notice a change in the sound of your voice and footsteps. When the house is empty, it has a hollow sound. The hard, exposed surfaces reflect and build up sound. A heavily draped and carpeted room will have a hushed quiet sound because of absorptions by the soft surfaces.

No two people will produce the same sounds. The resulting sounds depend on the size and shape of the cavities. Even the size and shape of the neck will influence the sounds.

Realizing the variations of the size and shape of these cavities, plus the thickness and tension of each structure, it is easy to imagine thousands of different sounds being produced. As Elton Abernathy puts it in a text book on speech, "With all these changes to ring up, he stamps his own personality onto his voice and marks it as distinct from the voice of any of his fellows, yet, at the same time; he produces innumerable variations of his own."

You have a general idea now where sound is being produced. It's in the "Adam's Apple." You can feel it on the outside of your throat. The pitch of your voice is governed by the number of double vibrations of the vocal fold per second. For a high pitch, you will need a fast rate of vibration. Of course, the length, thickness, and tension of the vocal cords also play a part in the pitch changes.

The loudness or intensity of your voice is caused by the force with which the air is being pushed through the vocal cords. Of course, this would place tension on the vocal cords as they open to release the air.

No matter what voice you are using, you will not want to talk so loud as to be offensive to others. Still, you will need to speak loud enough to be heard. Ask friends and classmates about your own voice. There are many factors that can cause one to speak too loudly without realizing it. The most common causes are faulty hearing and lack of confidence.

The quality of the voice is also governed by the vibrations of the vocal cords. Resonance plays a large part in producing the quality of the voice. The quality or timbre of your voice can be improved, and in most cases needs to be.

In order to have a good, clear, pleasing tone, you must have a relaxed throat. It takes only a few seconds to think into your throat and feel the relaxation take place.

A good tone is necessary if you are going to speak and entertain other people. When you begin to speak, your true personality comes forth. Your voice and speech not only reveals your intellectual background, they hint of your physical and mental well-being.

Practice for a Clear Voice

When you are performing before an audience, your voice is on display. Most likely your voice will be heard over a loud speaker. If you have unpleasant qualities in your voice, they will be magnified.

One way to improve your voice quality is to be aware at all times of what you are saying and how you are saying it. Listen to yourself talk. Do you like what you hear? Be certain to give every vowel and every consonant that should be sounded its full amount of attention. Be aware of the enunciation of the "B," "P," "T," and "D," and keep it crisp and clean. Sustain the "M," "N," and "NG" sounds slightly.

According to Elizabeth Ferguson von Hess, in her book, *So To Speak*, the "M," "N," and "NG" are the singing sounds. She suggests, and I agree with her, that you should hang on to these singing sounds, ever so slightly, when they occur in your speech.

You can feel these sounds being resonated in the nasal cavities. Place your forefinger and your thumb lightly on each side of the upper bridge of your nose. Slowly, say the "M," "N," and "NG" sounds, and notice the vibrations on your thumb and forefinger as the sounds are being resonated.

It is important to have a good normal speaking voice. In order to have a pleasant and clear voice, you must practice. And when you practice you need to employ extreme activity of the lips, tongue, and lower jaw. Then, when you speak in ordinary conversation, you should notice some crisp sounds and also at times a smooth slowness in your speech.

The overly emphasized activities of the lips, tongue, and lower jaw will also help develop the contrast between your facial movements when you speak and when your dummy speaks.

When you and your dummy are on stage and you speak, you need to look like you are speaking. When your dummy speaks, you need to look like you are listening. (Of course, when your dummy speaks, it needs to look like it's speaking. We will cover that subject in another chapter.)

Now to give the appropriate vowels and consonants their full amount of attention, read the following poem, by Jean Ingelow. (Remember to keep the "B," "P," "T," and "D" sounds crisp and clear, and to sustain the "M," "N," and "NG" sounds slightly.)

SEVEN TIMES ONE

There's no dew left on the daisies and clover,
    There's no rain left in heaven.
I've said my "seven times" over and over,
    Seven times one are seven.

I am old—so old I can write a letter;
    My birthday lessons are done.
The lambs play always—they know no better;
    They are only one times one.

O Moon! in the night I have seen you sailing
    And shining so round and low.
You were bright-ah, bright—but your light is failing;

You are nothing now but a bow.

You Moon! Have you done something wrong in heaven,
    That God has hidden your face?
I hope, if you have, you will soon be forgiven,
    And shine again in your place.

O velvet Bee! You're a dusty fellow,
    You've powdered your legs with gold.
O brave marsh Mary-buds, rich and yellow,
    Give me your money to hold!

O Columbine! open your folded wrapper.
    Where two twin turtle-doves dwell!
O Cuckoo-pint! tell me the purple clapper
    That hangs in your clear green bell!
And show me your nest, with the young ones in it,
    I will not steal them away;
I am old! you may trust me, linnet, linnet!
    I am seven times one to-day.
                JEAN INGELOW

Exercise for Voice Contrast

To encourage and help me form the habit of opening my mouth when I talked or sang, my vocal teacher Mrs. Benkley, from Nashville, Tennessee. taught me the following exercises. It seemed that while performing with the dummy for so many years I had gotten in the habit of talking with my lips only, leaving my jaw still. So, to further activate and exaggerate the movements of the facial muscles, try saying the following words. Stretch the lips and over-emphasize the sounds.

NOTE: It is recommended that you apply face cream around your mouth area before practicing the following words, as the exaggerated movements may stretch the skin.

"HIGH"
The first word is "High."

When saying the word "high," be sure to stretch the mouth open very tall. "High" - "high" - "high." Feel the sound in the roof of the mouth. "High" - "high" - "high." Think tall in the mouth. And practice, practice, and practice some more.

"WIDE"
The second word is "Wide."

Now say the word "wide," while spreading your mouth from ear to ear. "Wide" - "wide" - "wide."

Now, try saying "high" and "wide," while keeping the contrast and stretch in each word. The high exaggerated movement for the word high and the wide exaggerated movement for the word wide. "High" and "wide." "High" and "wide." "High" and "wide."

"ROUND"
The third word is "Round."

When saying the word "round," open the mouth as wide and high as possible, making the mouth form into a large circle. Say "round" slowly and fill up your mouth with sound. "Round" - "round" - "round."

Now put the three exercises together, keeping the distinct exaggerated mouth movements for each word. "High" - "high" - "high" - "wide" - "wide" - "wide" - "round" - "round" - "round."

"DO"
The forth word is "Do."

Say the word "do." Make it a very long, drawn-out "do-o-o." Pucker the lips in an exaggerated kiss fashion. Try to push the sound out of your mouth. You should feel the vibrations on your lips as the air passes through them. Remember to push your lips out in an exaggerated kiss fashion. "Do" - "do" - "do."

And finally practice putting all four exercises together saying them exaggerated and slow. "High" - "wide" - "round" - "do." Then speed them up until you are saying them as fast as possible, while still using the exaggerated movements.

I am sorry that we cannot fully describe, or pretend to explain, all of the qualities of the normal voice in this chapter. I would advise you to go to the local library if you are interested in learning more about voice production and voice projection. You will find some excellent books available. Everything that you learn about voice and speech will add to your success as a ventriloquist.

Chapter 4

STRENGTHENING THE TONGUE MUSCLES

Tongue Control

The tongue not only helps us to taste and chew, but also helps us to form sounds. The tongue is controlled to a small degree by moving the lower jaw, to which it is attached.

In spite of its attachment to the lower jaw, the tongue is mobile and versatile. The tongue has a network of intrinsic muscles running lengthwise, crosswise, and vertically, as well as multiple extrinsic muscular attachments, and it can be humped, curled, grooved, pointed, and flattened.

By learning to control the many groups of muscles of the tongue early in this course, you will become a better ventriloquist. You will be able to pronounce the hard letters and words more clearly. This could make the difference between your having excellent, as opposed to mediocre, ventrilocution.

First, you will learn to strengthen the different groups of muscles. Start by sticking out your tongue and trying to make it thin and pointed. Try to make the tongue resemble a pencil. Stick your tongue out as far as is comfortable. This won't be very far the first few times, but keep trying. Now hang your head until your chin touches your chest. Let your tongue fall out as far as you can. Let it hang loosely for a few seconds. Next, move your tongue from side to side fast and loose.

Second, try to touch your nose with your tongue. Then, again, hang your head and wiggle your tongue loosely from side to side. Do the same loose wiggle after you try to touch your chin with tongue. Now, try to touch one ear and then the other ear with the tongue. And, like before, hang your head and wiggle your tongue loosely from side to side. Be careful not to overdo the exercises; take only a few minutes each day.

You can notice the relationship of the tongue to the soft palate and hard palate. The tongue presses against these to produce different sounds.

When you start using the ventriloquial voice and mastering still lips, the tongue will have to work overtime. To get an idea of the difference it will make, say "ventriloquism." Now hold your lips still and say "ventriloquism." Notice how much harder your tongue had to work?

The Limber Tongue

To speak difficult words in a ventriloquous fashion, you will need a limber tongue. Many years ago, Charles Norman Granville, of Chicago, recognized this need. He was not a ventriloquist; he was a singing teacher. To help his students limber up their tongues, he wrote a rhythm and set it to music. The resulting song is "Tommy Tucker."

Just reading "Tommy Tucker" is very good for limbering up the tongue, and it's a fun exercise. Try it any time your tongue feels thick or clumsy.

TOMMY TUCKER

Lit-tle Tom-my Tuck-er was a fun-ny lit-tle chap
    whose dad-dy was a sail-or on the bay.
Oh his tongue-tied tongue was tied in a knot,
    so he could-n't sing for sup-per so they say.
But a-long came a friend from the ci-ty of Penn,
    and a piece of good ad-vice he gave;
Say-ing: Tom-my if you want to get your tongue
un-tied, Why! Kay-gle, Oh-gle, Aye-gle, Oh-gle Aye.

Kay-gle, Oh-gle, Aye-gle, Oh-gle, Aye-gle, Oh-gle
Kay-gle, Oh-gle, Aye-gle, Oh-gle, Aye-gle, Oh-gle

Kay-gle, Oh-gle, Aye-gle, Oh-gle, Aye-gle, Oh-gle
Kay-gle, Oh-gle, Aye-gle, Oh-gle, Aye.

It's a fun thing to sing this poem to any tune that comes to your mind. And it will always relax the tongue, mouth, and throat. So, try it. You may want to try and see if your dummy can sing "Tommy Tucker" later on.

Now that we've gotten a limber tongue, and are doing our best to strengthen the tongue muscles, let's work on our breathing.

Chapter 5

FIRST STEPS TO VENTRILOQUIZING

Controlled Breathing

The word "ventriloquism" comes from two Latin words, *venter*, meaning "belly," and *loquail*, meaning "to speak." This is where the Greeks got the name "belly prophets." Their belief that ventriloquists talked from the stomach was partly true; to speak in a ventriloquial voice takes excellent control of the stomach muscles. These muscles are used in expelling the right amount of air, at the right time, through the vocal cords. Controlled breathing is one of the first steps to becoming a ventriloquist.

Concentrate your attention on the use of the stomach muscles for strong, controlled exhalation. Place your right hand on your abdomen, your left hand on your chest. Say "ha" in a quick, staccato fashion four times, pressing in steadily with your right hand. Repeat the exercise, letting the abdomen muscles do the pushing inward, and letting your right hand merely follow and feel the inward movement.

Breath enters through the mouth and nose, travels down the throat, into the trachea, down through bronchial tubes, filling little lung-cells. Breath returns through the same channels.

Try saying a series of slow syllables like "ha, ha, ha." Starting and stopping by the inward movement of the abdominal muscles and the downward movement of the

36

diaphragm. Do not use the laryngeal valve to start and stop the air stream.

Another good exercise is to stand straight, arms at your sides, looking straight ahead. Now, inhale slowly as you turn your head slowly to the left. Hold for 5 seconds as you look over your left shoulder. Exhale slowly as you turn your head to the front. Inhale as you slowly move head to the right side. Hold for 5 seconds as you look over right shoulder. Exhale slowly as you return head to normal position.

This exercise promotes better breathing habits, and also helps to limber the neck. It is important for ventriloquists to have a limber neck, as they have to look often to the side at the dummy. You want this movement to look natural.

The Key to "Throwing the Voice"

By now, you know that the chief muscles for controlled breathing are in the abdominal area. The diaphragm is the large muscle above the abdominal cavity. As you breathe in, the dome of the diaphragm moves downward. This increases the space in the chest cavity, and the expansion creates a negative vacuum inside the cavity, causing outside air to rush into the lungs.

By using the diaphragm and stomach muscles to control the flow of air as we are exhaling, we create the ventriloquial voice.

The reason that we are talking about controlled breathing instead of trying to find the ventriloquial voice is that, by controlling the amount of air passing through the vocal cords, we create our ventrilocution, which is your voice for your dummy.

One of my students found this out for himself when he was saying "hello" to his "genie" in the bottle, and he dropped the bottle and it rolled under the couch. As he bent over to get the bottle, he said "hello" and to his surprise the word "hello" came out sounding like a distance voice. Like a voice that could have been down in a bottle. What had happened was that when he bent over from the waist to look under the couch, he put pressure on the diaphragm. This pressure forced the air through the vocal cords at a greater force than usual.

Try it yourself and feel the difference. Say "hello" in your normal voice. Now bend over, as you would to look under a chair, and say "hello" again. Notice that you are forcing a small amount of air through the lungs by putting upward pressure on your diaphragm. Now stand up and say "hello," using your stomach muscles to help push the word out. Feel the muscles go in as you say the word, "hello." It is almost as if you are talking with your stomach.

Try saying small words like no, no, no. Place your hands on your stomach and feel the muscles tighten. Do not do this more than 10 minutes or you may have some sore muscles tomorrow. So, please, take it easy. You have just said your first ventriloquistic words. Maybe? You'll know later if you got them out correctly or not.

If you have ever taken vocal lessons, you know the value of controlled breathing habits. Here again, I ask you to learn as much about proper breathing as you can. There isn't room in these lessons for all the things I would like to share with you. You may want to learn more on proper breathing at your local library.

Chapter 6

YOUR VENTRILOCUTION

It's No Big Deal

By now, you know that the ventriloquial voice is no big deal. In other words, it is one of the easiest parts of being a ventriloquist. At this time, you are not trying to get a voice that is coming from the ceiling or from the floor—you only need a voice that will sound one or two feet away from you. If you can do this, and at the same time give the voice a little different tonal quality, you are in business.

A lot of mystery has been placed around the ventriloquist. One of the reasons for this is that some ventriloquists don't want other people to learn, so they try to make it hard. They make the lessons too difficult to understand. This was especially true in the 1800s.

I prefer Paul Winchell and Jimmy Nelson's methods of acquiring the ventriloquial voice to other methods. They are very similar to the one my student accidently learned when he dropped the genie bottle and said "AH" as he bent over to pick it up.

So, now in a seated position, say the word "AH" and as you say it, lean over with your hand on your diaphragm, pressing gently. At the same time try to hold back on the air, making it a little harder to get the word out.

Now fill up your lungs and say a long drawn out "AHHHHHH." Lean forward again, and try to sustain the "AH," making it "AH H H." Try to bounce the sound back in your throat not straight out your mouth. Soon, this may sound like a bee drone, or a grunting drone. The drone is what it is all about. It is what you are looking for. You are looking for an "AH" that sounds something like a far away bee drone. Now, as you say "AH" lean forward with your hand on your diaphragm, pushing gently. Say "AH" over and over. You must practice until you can find a drone sound easily. And then you start trying to give voice to the drone.

One book that I read once called it a grunt. Instead of saying just "AH" or grunting, you can now go on to the "bah" of a sheep. Try to make them sound right beside you, and then a few feet away. Next, try to make the "caw" of a crow.

Fred T. Darvill, author of *How to Become a Ventriloquist*, says the next step should be the vowels, and I agree with him. So now substitute the "AHs" and the "BAHs" and the "CAWs" with the vowels. Start with "A" and when you've got it down pat, go on to "E," "I," "O," and "U." There is nothing hard about this. Before you start saying other words, you must learn all the letters of the alphabet.

The Beginner's Alphabet

You are now ready to ventriloquize. Produce the drone sound, and give voice to it. Again say the sounds of "aw", "caw," "baw," and all of the vowels. Make them sound as if they are different from your normal voice.

There are only 15 letters left in the 20 letter beginner's alphabet for you to learn. You have started with the five vowels—"A," "E," "I," "O," and "U"—and for the moment, we are omitting the five troublesome letters: "B," "F," "M," "P," and "V." We will be dealing with these problem letters later in this chapter. And we will also deal with "W" later.

Now, sit in front of a mirror. Relax. Open your mouth slightly. Your teeth should be almost touching, but not quite. Do not grit your teeth. Keep your lips relaxed and normal looking. In this position, say the letters that we call the beginners alphabet, using the drone sound. And don't forget to let your stomach help get the sound out. Feel the muscles working for you.

Say the beginner's alphabet now. "C - D - G - H - J - K - L - N - Q - R - S - T - X - Y – Z."

Now, put them all together and practice until you feel that you can say each letter without moving your lips.

"A - C - D - E - G - H - I - J - K - L - N - O - Q - R - S - T - U - X - Y - Z."

Here I am assuming that you are trying to make these 20 letters sound different from your normal voice. But don't be too hard on yourself. You can always back-track and read this chapter again. A little time and practice will help you digest this new information and enable you to use it better.

The Labials or "Troublesome" Letters

The word "labial" means "of the lip." This is why we call the following letters labials. They cannot be said easily without lip movement. Up to now, you have been using only 20 letters of the alphabet. Now it's time to tackle the five labials, or troublesome letters: "B," "F," "M," "P," "V." If there is anything hard about ventriloquism, I would say it is learning how to say these five letters without lip movement. There are all kinds of schools of thought on this subject. But Paul Winchell has what is to me the quickest and simplest method. I keep referring to Paul because it was through his book, *The Key To Ventriloquism*, that I learned the near ventriloquial voice.

I checked his book out of the library one day many years ago. The next week, I ordered myself a dummy from a mail-order catalogue. The dummy arrived on a Wednesday, and on the following Saturday night I performed my first ventriloquial show with my new dummy, which I called "Little Joe." It was family night at our local church, and from that performance, I was invited to do two more shows the following week. I have never stopped performing after that night.

Back to the letters "B," "F," "M," "P," and "V." Ventriloquists before us have paved the way and made saying these letters very easy. You just use substitutes for the hard letters.

The Letters "F" and "V"

For "F," use the soft "TH" sound like in the words "think" and "thank."

For the "V," substitute the hard "TH" sound like in "those" and "these." Paul gives us an example: "Very funny." Try saying "very funny," keeping in mind the fact that you use the soft "TH" sound of "think" or "thank" for the letter "F," and the hard "TH" sound for the "V" from "these" or "those." If written, it would look like this: "thery thunny." Of course, you have to practice and practice until "thery thunny" comes out "very funny." Notice here that the tongue is working overtime as you are trying to keep a still lip.

Jimmy Nelson, the famous ventriloquist we used to see on the Nestle's Chocolate commercials with his dog, Farfel, is a strong believer in thinking one thing while you say another. Let me explain this. You say "thery thunny" using the "TH" sound while you are thinking "very funny." In other words, you are saying "thery thunny," while thinking "very funny." With practice, this method of Jimmy Nelson's will work like a charm.

Now you are ready to practice from a list of words and phrases using the troublesome letters "V" and "F." The dictionary will come in handy for this. Here is a list that I came up with and you can add to it.

Practice words for the letter "F"

Using the soft sound of "TH," like in the words "think" and "thank," as a substitute for the letter "F" practice the following words.

face	fade
fair	faith
fall	fancy
fast	fat
feast	feed
feel	fetch
fever	fish
flag	flight
flirt	flower
flush	foggy
foil	fold
follow	food
foolish	foot
force	fork
fountain	fox
French	fresh
friend	frog
fun	fur
furry	fuzzy

Practice phrases for the letter "F"

1. The faded flower fluttered and fell.

2. The fellow felt very foolish when he found the frog in the fountain.

3. The foolish fellow followed a fancy footed friend and fell flat on the floor.

4. The fellow wanted fox fur for a fall felt coat.

Practice words for the letter "V"

Substituting the hard "TH" sound like in "those" and "these" for the letter "V" practice saying the following words.

vacancy	valet
valley	value
van	vase
velvet	venison
venture	ventriloquist
vestment	vice
victory	vigor
village	villain
view	vintage
violet	vitality
vivacious	vocal
voice	vote
vowel	vulgar
vulture	

Practice phrases for the letter "V"

1. The foolish venture investment turned out very good.

2. Vocal exercises are a good tool in the victory of voice.

3. The velvet vested vulgar vice ridden villain ran.

4. The violet vase was seen in Vincent Van Gogh's art.

The Letters "P," "B," and "M"

Most ventriloquists agree on the substitutions for these three letters. But first, say the letters the way you normally do "P," "B," "M." Notice the lip movement it takes to form these three letters. That's why they are called labials (meaning "of the lips"). Don't despair—you can learn to say these words in a different way. My Aunt Geraldine always says, "There is more than one way to skin a cat," and she was right. You will just substitute "easy to say" letters for these three "troublesome" letters, and relearn them.

Substitutions for "P," "B," and "M"

Substitute the "T" sound for "P."
Substitute the "D" sound for "B."
substitute the "N" sound for "M."

Repeat these substitute letters until they are, as the old timers would say, burned in your mind like letters of fire on the wall. The substitute letters are "T," "D," and "N." These are formed normally with the tongue touching the roof of the mouth slightly behind the upper teeth. Now to form these letters, "T," "D," "N," and make them sound like "P," "B," "M," push the tongue forward against the upper teeth.

Substitute the Letter "T" for the Letter "P"

Now try saying the substitute letter "T" with the tongue pushed against the upper teeth lightly. First, say "T" with the new tongue position and as you say "T," think "P." Remember what Jimmy Nelson taught us: think one letter while saying another. Try it over and over with the new tongue position. Keep a still lip but not a stiff lip, and relax. When you are satisfied with the sound, go on to the next "troublesome" letter.

Practice Words for the Letter "P"

Practice the following words and sentences using the substitute letter "T" for the letter "P." Again think "P" and say "T" with the tongue pushed against the upper teeth lightly.

pace	pack
pad	paddle
paddy	page
paid	pain
paint	pair
palace	pan
panel	paper
parish	parrot
parsley	part
partial	particular
party	pass
passion	past
paste	pastry
patch	patent
path	patience
patient	paw

pay	peace
pedigree	peep
peg	pen
pencil	penny
people	personal
picket	picture
pigeon	pillow
pin	pinch
pink	pint
pitcher	pizza
pony	prince

Practice Phrases for the Letter "P"

1. Peter Piper picked a peck of pickled peppers.

2. If Peter Piper picked a peck of pickled peppers, where's the peck of pickled peppers Peter Piper picked.

3. The pink panther panted because the parrot pecked his nose.

4. Paul painted the palace peach and pink.

5. Paddy Paws pussy footed past the patient panhandler.

Substitute the Letter "D" for the Letter "B"

Now, let's try a new tongue position for the letter "B." Press the tongue lightly against the upper teeth. Say the letter "D" while thinking "B." Do this over and over again with the new tongue position. Say it until you are sure it is coming out sounding like "B."

Practice Words for the Letter "B"

Practice the following words and sentences using the substitute letter "D" for the letter "B." Remember, practice makes perfect. And this substitution may not come easy, but, just keep on practicing. You can do it. Think "B" while saying the "D." Use the new tongue position and relax. It will happen if you practice long enough and have that burning desire to be a ventriloquist.

babble	baboon
baby	back
bad	badge
baffle	bag
baggage	bait
bakery	bald
ball	balloon
ballerina	band
banquet	bat
bath	beach
beauty	bed
behind	bell
bet	big
bill	bingo
bird	birthday
black	blanket
block	blonde
blue	boa
boat	body
boost	born
boss	brain
break	breath
bribe	bride

bright	bring
brother	buffer
bug	buggy
bully	burn
busy	button
buy	by

Practice Phrases for the Letter "B"

1. The new born black sheep, went baa, baa.

2. The little boy's big brother played the bag pipe in the band.

3. She was busy painting big blue balloons on the blackboard.

4. The bully pushed a baby buggy down the block to the bingo board.

Substitute the Letter "N" for the Letter "M"

Now, let's go on and try the letter "M" in the same manner. Substitute the letter "N" for the letter "M" using the new tongue position, with the tongue pushed against the upper teeth lightly. Practice saying the "N" over and over with the new tongue position while thinking "M" until it comes out sounding like "M." Remember what Jimmy Nelson taught us; say one sound, while thinking another.

Practice Words for the Letter "M"

Practice the following words and sentences using the substitute letter "N" for the letter "M." Remember, practice makes perfect.

macaroon	machine
mad	maid
main	makeup
mammy	man
mantle	map
march	match
may	meow
merry	milk
mind	mink
molasses	money
mood	moon
morning	moss
motor	mouth
mud	muff
mug	mule
mum	mush
myself	mystic
myth	

Practice Phrases for the Letter "M"

1. The man tried to sell the main machine for more money.

2. The milk maid tried to milk a cow, but it was a mule.

3. The cat meowed because he fell in the mud.

4.   Many men make molasses, but mammy made mush from corn.

The Letter "W"

Now, let's talk about the letter "W." Some people have trouble saying the letter "W" because of the "B" sound in the "double yoo," so, we will treat the "B" like before and substitute "D" while thinking "B." This takes a little practice, but you will soon find it works.

When you use "W" in a word, it is usually pronounced "wah." Take the words, "when," "which," and "where." You don't say "W" or "double yoo," you use the "wuh" sound. So if you have trouble with the "W" sound, substitute "OO." Like the OO sound like in moon. Thus making "when" (OOEN) and "where" (OOAR).

Practice Words and Phrases for the Letter "W"

wad	wade
waffle	wag
wage	wagon
waist	walk
waltz	want
ward	ware
warm	warrant
wash	waste
water	wave
wax	weak
weave	webbing
weight	well
west	what

wheel	when
where	which
while	whip
wish	white
why	wide
wiggle	wild
will	wind
window	wing
wire	wise
wish	wonder
word	work

Practice Phrases for the Letter "W"

1. She waltzed on the dance floor, but walked off when she saw that her partner waddled like a duck.

2. It was the worst waffle; the waiter with the white apron had ever whipped up.

3. Was she wrong to wonder why she had to work while she waited for the wagon?

4. The wind blew in the window and blew water on the waxed floor.

I will just stop here and impress upon you the importance of practice. There are thousands of people who know the troublesome letter substitutes. This is not a well-kept secret. But for all the thousands who have this knowledge, only a few have the dedication it takes to become a skilled ventriloquist. Most people aren't disciplined enough to force themselves to sit down in front of a mirror and practice. So practice, practice, practice, and then practice some more.

Synchronization of Sound and Movement

Up until now, we have been so busy that we haven't talked much about using your sock puppet when you practice. So, now, get out the sock puppet; it is very important that you start early in training your brain to know when you want to speak, and when you want the dummy voice to come out. So, from now on, when you practice, be sure that the hand puppet's mouth opens at the same time as the ventriloquistic voice sounds come out. Move the puppet's mouth slightly for each syllable— make sure you have perfect synchronization between the ventriloquial voice and hand movement.

Now, with your list of words and phrases using the letters "B," "V," "F," "M," "P," and "W" you are ready to practice with the puppet. Always sit in front of a mirror or use a hand mirror so that you can keep a close watch on your lip movement. Practice the same word over and over until there is not even the slightest quiver of the lips.

When you are on TV, the slightest movements of the lips show up. The slight quiver of the lip as air passes through is clearly seen in close-up shots.

Besides going over the lists of words and phrases that we have made, here are some other things you can do to practice. Read books of poems, read the daily newspaper, or use any other reading material. Alternate the ventriloquial voice and the normal voice. If you are a singer, add songs to this list. Whatever else you do, practice. You can practice as you drive down the road to work. You can practice in the shower, you can practice in the tub, and you can practice while you cook. But you always need the practice times when you can sit down in front of a mirror.

Another good way to learn to imitate the ventriloquial voice is to hear and watch other ventriloquists work. Watch the newspapers for ventriloquists appearing in your area. You can study their timing and the sound of their ventriloquial voice. Most good ventriloquists will be happy to answer questions for you after the show. But don't be discouraged if they give you the brush-off.

There are some ventriloquists who are not secure enough to help others, but just watching them perform will be a big help. Take mental notes or take a little tablet and take real notes on how the performers get on and off stage. Keep your eyes open; you can always learn from other performers.

At first, you should limit your practice sessions to about 10 to 15 minutes each. It is far better to practice for 10 to 15 minutes four times a day than for one hour at one sitting. I am talking about the beginner. After your throat muscles are strong, and you have been practicing on a regular basis for some time, you can practice as long as you want.

A warm cup of tea or coffee will help soothe the muscles and relieve soreness. In many older books on ventriloquism, it is often suggested you drink hot water with lemon and honey in it. I've tried this and it is very good.

Now I caution you again to take it gentle and easy. Practice only a short time and then rest.

Chapter 7

WHEN THE DUMMY TALKS
Type of Voice

Before you can decide what type of voice you want, you must know what dummy is going to use the voice. Before you know what dummy you want to buy, you must know what voice is the best for you to use; what voice you do best. So, it's a toss-up as to which should be first, picking a voice or finding a partner. I choose "type of voice" because some people have a limited amount of "voices" to choose from. Also, some people find they have a natural voice for a young kid or a perfect voice for an older lady, etc. By finding your type of ventriloquial voice first; it will help you when picking a dummy. The three qualities that make a voice distinctive are intensity, pitch, and quality (timbre).

1. **Intensity** is the volume, and it is governed by the force of air passing through the voice box. Breathing exercises will help to control the intensity of your voice.

2. **Pitch** is how high or low your voice is on the scale. If your own voice is low on the scale, you will try to place your dummy's voice high. Women with a high voice should try to use a low voice for their dummy. Try to pitch your voice to receive the maximum amount of contrast between your voice and the voice you want for your dummy.

3.   **Quality** or timbre is the dimension of your voice. Is it smooth, gentle, piercing or shrill? Practice will do a lot to make the quality the way you want it.

You Need Contrast

Again, think of what you want the voice to sound like and try to imitate it. You must think, in your throat, exactly how you want your dummy to sound. Make sure you do not get an unpleasant voice. There are a very few people who, for medical reasons, are unable to obtain a voice with as much contrast as they would like.

I know one man whose voice was low and he was unable to get a high voice for his dummy. In a case such as this, I would recommend a different tempo. If you have a dumb-boy dummy or an alligator, a slow voice works fine. Try to get as much contrast as possible, and then slow down the tempo. Slowing down the tempo will create more contrast. A witty kid, an old woman, etc., could have a fast tempo, thus creating more contrast from your own voice.

Another good way to achieve maximum contrast is to give your dummy an accent. I have a character named Carlos who speaks with a Spanish accent. This puts him in a different class. His voice doesn't resemble any other character I use. Of course, only one can have the accent: either you or the dummy. It is more fun for the dummy to speak with the accent.

Remember to use your hand puppet; so your voice will be synchronized with its mouth movements. Now practice singing up the scale: do-re-me-fa-so-la-ti-do, and down again: do-ti-la-so-fa-me-re-do. Do this using your ventriloquial voice. Stop at intervals on the scale and try speaking dialogue. Practice every possible placement for the voice. You will really be surprised at what you can do; most people are unaware of the wide range of different sounds they can produce. Don't be afraid someone will laugh at you, when you make those funny sounds. Actually that's what this is all about, getting laughs.

Another way to help decide on a voice is to copycat. Listen to comedians on TV, radio, or old records. The older the better. Find one you like and try to imitate it. There is nothing unethical about this method.

1. The voice is for the dummy, not you, and the style of speaking is for the dummy.

2. Even if you tried your best, you could not come recognizably close to matching your ventrolocution to someone else's voice.

3. So, you see you may copy cat, but it will come out pleasantly different, and all yours. Try it.

When practicing a song that the dummy is going to sing, be sure the dummy is present.

When the voice is matched with a dummy, and you are actually practicing with one, the voice will come out more distinct.

The voice you choose should be pleasant to the ear, and easy on your throat. Never use a voice if it is scratchy, or irritates your throat. Spend the next week or two just trying out different voices. Think about different dummies and try to place a voice with them.

Chapter 8

THE GREAT MOMENT

Picking a Dummy

The great moment has arrived. You are ready to choose a partner. Until now, you have been using a hand puppet. But you have progressed past the hand puppet stage. You are now ready for a full-sized professional dummy or full-sized professional puppet.

You will probably want your main dummy to be a person, like a man, woman, boy or girl. They will wear better with the audience. The novelties and animals are great to have, but only to bring out to break up the program and create enthusiasm and add variety.

My first dummy was small, but I wasn't sure what I wanted in a dummy and at that time I didn't know where to find professional dummies. But this was a start and that's all I needed. My little dummy, Joe Wood, had a string in the back of his neck. His head did not move and his eyes did not move.

Hand Puppets

Let me make something clear here. I didn't mean you have progressed past the professional puppet stage, only past the small play puppets and sock puppets. There are many puppets that are perfect for professional entertaining. Sometimes, the only difference between the professional and the play puppet is size. A professional puppet must be large enough to be seen from the back of an auditorium.

Hand puppets differ in price, depending on size, moving parts, and type of material used to make them. One thing you must have in a hand puppet is a moving mouth. A puppet is no good for ventriloquism if its mouth doesn't move.

Many hand puppets have legs and arms. Your hand goes in through the back of the neck or up through its bottom. Some hand puppets are as large as a full-size professional dummy.

In the puppet line, you have a variety of types to choose from. The dog and the bear seem to be a favorite with audiences of all ages. I once used a routine in which my dummy had an imaginary dog. We would drop a book off the table and hit the dog. You could hear the dog go yelping off of the stage. Many grown-ups as well as children have asked me if they could see my little brown and white dog. They remember seeing it, even though we didn't have one. So you can see that dogs are a favorite. But, here again, you wouldn't want to use an animal all the time, because "people dummies" wear better.

Jimmy Nelson's dog Farfel is another living proof of the success of dogs. Children much too young to remember the old Nestle's Chocolate commercial know Farfel and ask him to do the commercial when he is entertaining. They knew him from hearing their parents speak of him. He is that famous, but still, Farfel the dog is not Jimmy's main character.

The cat is a very sweet animal, but hasn't had much success as a famous puppet. But you could be the one to change that. Don't be afraid to try new things, no matter what I tell you.

Other good hand puppets include the lion, tiger, frog, rabbit, and best of all boys and girls with big mouths.

I once had a rabbit hand puppet. It had a head, arms and sleeve body that came to my elbow and I could put my hand up the sleeve and out into his mouth. The first thing I did to the rabbit after I purchased it was change his appearance. So he would not look like every other rabbit sold by the same person. First I sewed sock legs on him; stuffed with cushion stuffing. Next, I sewed big pink felt feet on the ends of the stuffed socks (tube socks). Then I bought him a pair of overalls. I named him "Paddy Paws" and used him that way for several years.

When we started the TV show, I changed him again. Paddy Paws became Billy Jack the royal farmer in the video "Three Days in the Palace." Also, in the TV series "King Joe's Palace." And Billy Jack is in the story book, "The Story Of Dummyland." To get Billy Jack ready for the TV show I found him a plaid shirt and a straw hat. But he stayed bare foot because of his cute big pink feet.

Yes, Billy Jack is one of my cutest characters. He's the royal farmer in my fantasy world of Dummyland. He has his own TV set with chickens, eggs, hay, flowers, barn, and more.

This is food for thought, and it proves that it's good to think ahead and try to visualize what all you can do with each character you choose.

Carved Dummies

If you want a hand-carved dummy, you need to get a list of the dummy carvers. Hand carved dummies are very expensive and the waiting list is usually long. I have been on one waiting list for several years. The wooden dummies are very durable and preferred by some ventriloquists.

The new fiberglass and plastic wood dummies are very nice. It takes a keen eye to tell them from the wooden ones. They are not as expensive as the wooden dummies.

The dummies mentioned above can be made to order. You decide what you want your dummy to look like and work out the details with the dummy maker. You will want to send along a picture of yourself so the maker can make the dummy's features opposite of yours. Like the voice, you will want as much contrast in looks as possible. There are so many ventriloquists with neat, smart kids that the trend is now moving toward the "real character dummies."

If you have your heart set on a real dummy, you must decide how much you want to pay and then shop around. Sometimes, it's hard to find dummies, so you get carried away and buy anything you're offered, so I'm telling you now don't buy the first dummy you see. They may be hard to find, but there are plenty around.

Moving Parts

What moving parts should your dummy have? Let's start with what it needs to be effective and then add what you want it to have. Your dummy must have two things: a moving head and a moving mouth. All else is optional. For years, Charley McCarthy had only a moving head and a moving mouth. A dummy with a moving mouth and head can charm an audience with his wit and personality. Too many moving parts and you "awe" the audience with the dummy's mechanics. And that makes you look like an amateur. Jimmy Nelson's famous Danny O'Day only has moving head, mouth and eyes.

The next thing you would add is moving eyes—from side to side. Next would be the closing eyes. This is all I would recommend on a dummy.

When you have too many controls, it takes time to work them, and you lose some of the life which the tilt, and twist of the pole gives the dummy.

It's usually the amateur that has to have "everything" on his dummy. There are over 25 moving parts to choose from: from a tongue that sticks out to a big toe that wiggles. I must mention the big belly that shakes when he laughs. You and you alone must decide on your dummy, and its moving parts. Usually your pocketbook will help you decide.

A few companies make a molded or standard dummy. Usually you have a choice of a dozen or more types. You can change the hair and clothes on these dummies, so not even the manufacturers would recognize it on sight.

Whatever you do, don't try to build or make your first dummy. It is just as dumb for a new ventriloquist to try to make his first dummy, as it would be for a pianist to try to make his first piano.

Dressing Your Dummy

Clothes are very important to your dummy. Don't be cheap when you go to buy its clothes. After all, it will be wearing them for a long time. Dress your dummy according to the personality you want it to project. Dummies are usually shipped with cheap clothing because manufacturers realize that the ventriloquist will want to change its clothes as soon as possible. It's a good idea to change the wig if you buy a molded stock figure. Then, your dummy won't look like every other dummy ordered from the same company.

If you can order your dummy without clothes and wig at a lower price, I would suggest you do just that. One thing to remember: when you open the package, you are in for a shock unless you are used to seeing naked, bald dummies. So don't send it packing back until you've seen a wig on its head and have it dressed.

Remember, dummies don't have to stay the way they are. Experiment with them, change their hair, eyebrows, beard, and clothes. Keep trying until you get them the way you want them. Even if you have a dummy with molded hair, you can still put a wig on it. A little Elmers Glue works wonders.

Once you get your dummy looking the way you want it to look, the voice will become more permanent and distinct. Its personality will develop. Once it has, don't use routines contrary to that personality.

Foley Brown, a dummy carver, made me a dummy that I called Uncle Nick. Uncle Nick helped me in school assembly shows for several years. Then, I seemed to run out of things for him to do or say. I changed my complete school assemble program every year, because I went to the most of the same schools each year and the same children would be seeing the show.

I wanted a different character, but I didn't want to buy a new dummy. And this is what I did: I bought a ladies wig and cut it to fit Uncle Nick's head. I found a child's dress that looked like it could be worn by an older lady. I bought a pair of knee high stockings and a pair of little shoes. And before you could say "Jack Robinson," Uncle Nick became Aunt Clara, the fortune teller. Having the dummy be the fortune teller is very funny.

Aunt Clara! Yes, Uncle Nick turned into a beautiful graceful elderly woman right before my eyes. When my friends asked where Uncle Nick went, I told them he went to New York City and had a sex change and came back as Aunt Clara. And he sure made a very nice Aunt Clara. I forgot to tell you that I added a little padding here and there to his body to finish out the transformation.

My son Martin's dummy is made in the likeness of a famous clown; you wouldn't want to change his clothes or image. You wouldn't even want to change his name. This dummy would need to stay Emmet.

My dummy is a one of a kind and it was carved by the well known actor, ventriloquist and dummy maker Alan Semok. You may have seen Alan in commercials with his dummy.

Chapter 9

BREATHING LIFE INTO THE DUMMY

The Dummy Is a Dummy

It may sound as if I am contradicting myself, telling you to breathe life into the dummy after telling you not to treat it as if it was a real person. I want you to realize it is a dummy—you know it is a dummy and the people know it's a dummy. So, don't try to pretend it is real, especially on stage.

Off stage, the dummy goes into the case. On stage, you give it life with your creative acting and illusion ability. What I'm trying to say is this: Even though you don't say the dummy is real "on stage," its action should be so good the audience will believe it is real for the moment, and love it.

Many ventriloquists talk about their dummies as if they are children, with real feelings, etc. The reason for this is that many teachers and older ventriloquists were taught, "Give your dummy a name and believe he is alive from then on. Never mention that you are a ventriloquist or that he is a dummy."

I do not believe in this method. As Jimmy Nelson once told me, "A dummy is a dummy and should go back in the case as soon as the performance is over." Many times in Nelson's performance he mentions the fact that he is doing the talking and that Danny is a dummy.

When Danny catches Nelson trying to strike a match on his wooden head, he exclaims, "What are you trying to do, make an ash out of me?" This statement says, "I'm made out of wood."

You only make yourself look childish and foolish when you try to fool a crowd of intelligent people into thinking your dummy is real. Small children will believe what they want to believe, no matter what you tell them. Like Santa, they know there isn't one, but still they pretend there is. No matter what you say, they will think the dummy is a real person if they want to. This doesn't mean you should, but you must keep the audience aware that you know he's a dummy. Otherwise, you will look like a schizophrenic. Older children will be hurt to think that you, the ventriloquist, think they are dumb, and will fall for a trick like that.

One church ventriloquist I know lets her husband introduce her, and he tells about their darling dummy as if it was an only child: how it acts at home and that it is now lost somewhere in the church. The dummy finally appears, but it is several minutes before you can forget the sick introduction and enjoy the ventriloquist's performance.

I think a dummy should look like a dummy. This adds depth and dimension to the illusion. There's nothing unusual about a little boy talking. But a dummy that looks like it's made of wood can enchant even the hardest of hearts when it talks. Sir George B. Shaw realized this when he wrote "P.S. Dolls and Puppets." He states

I always hold up the wooden actors as instruction object-lessons to our flesh-and-blood players. The wooden ones, though stiff and continually glaring at you with the same overcharged expression, move you as only the most experienced living actors can. What really affects us in the theater is not the muscular activities of the performers, but the feelings they awaken in us by their aspect; for the imagination of the spectator plays a far greater part there than the exertions of the actors. The puppet is the actor in his primitive form.

Don't Covet the Art

My theory: the dummy becomes real as soon as you set it on your knee, just as an actress becomes the character she is portraying as soon as the curtain goes up. When the curtain closes, she is not the character any longer. Likewise, the dummy should go into the case immediately after a performance. But if I see a person who has a burning desire to see the dummy and waits long after the crowd is gone trying to get a glimpse of it, I could never leave without letting the child or grown-up see the dummy again. I have never tried to covet the art or any of the sources of my knowledge. I have always had private students and was the first to teach ventriloquism at a college level.

I once watched a young lady give a beautiful religious performance. The superintendent of the church took up a free will offering for her. After church, he gave her the money. The wad so was so big, she couldn't hold it all in one hand. There was a young girl standing by, watching. She was about 14 years old and very much overweight. "Could I have a last look at Billy? I've always wanted to be a ventriloquist, and don't know how to start."

"No, he's in bed for the night," was the stern reply. Now a girl of 14 doesn't wait that long after the crowd is gone to see a dummy unless she has a keen interest in the art. I couldn't get that incident out of my mind. So, the next day, I contacted the pastor of the church and asked for the girl's name. I wanted to give her the chance to see a real dummy and learn to throw her voice if she wanted to, but the pastor had no idea who the girl was.

But I still believe that the visiting ventriloquist should have taken the time to talk to the young lady. But she had her money and she hurried off, not caring if she hurt other people's feelings. Forgive me if sometimes I get off the subject. There is so much I want to share with you, and I know I can't get it all in this one book, but I still keep trying. Now, let's get on to breathing life into the dummy.

Get the Most out of Your Dummy

From the moment the curtain goes up, or you walk out in front of an audience, make the dummy alive. Do this with actions, actions, actions. You can refer to it as many times as you want as a dummy, but it will still be real to the audience. Start moving the dummy as soon as it comes into the view of the audience. Never let it hang limp.

Many times when I am performing, the dummy sits on my knee. With a little movement on the ball of the foot, I can get a lot of action from the dummy.

But if you are standing or walking, hold your dummy on your hand and you can get in a lot of body action. But the knee position is even better. Put your foot on a stool or chair. Sit the dummy back so its bottom is largely over the back of your leg. This allows you to control the body with just a twist of the knee. Rest the weight of your leg on the ball of your foot. With a little practice, even you will see it come alive. Always practice in front of a mirror.

If you have to work from a stand, you limit the actions of the dummy's body. There are times when this is the only way you can work. I do one act where my main dummy acts as master of ceremonies of the evening. Of course, I have to leave him and do other things and then go back to him. So he needs to be sitting on a stand. If you plan to work from a stand, then practice from a stand. The stand should be at a comfortable height. The dummy's face should be about even with yours; you shouldn't have to look down or up to it. If you are not using the dummy, turn its face away from the audience. This way, it is not staring blankly at them.

My friend Col. Bill Boley has a dummy named Aunt Fanny. Aunt Fanny sits on a stand. Bill does a wonderful job. I've seen Bill work many times and the stand works great for him.

Actions for Your Dummy

Angry: Lift the dummy's head slightly and lean it forward. Turn its head toward you, as if it were staring at you.

Excited: Move dummy's body up and down and open its mouth.

Sick: Hang its head to one side, maybe even to the point of laying it on your shoulder.

Surprised: Push dummy's head up out of collar and open the mouth wide—all quick actions.

Speechless: Give body and head a little rocking motion.

Keeping time to music: The side-to-side motion is best for this.

Sleep: If the dummy has moving eyes, sleep is no problem; if not, turn its head away from audience and suggest it's sleeping—it may lay its head on your shoulder.

Sexy look: Give the body a rolling motion and open its mouth a little, depending on size of the dummy.

Agree: We all know how to make a dummy agree with what we are saying by moving its head up and down, slowly if it is not too excited about the subject, and fast if anxiously agreeing.

Disagree: Move its head from side to side. If the dummy is being dramatic about the issue move its head firmly but slowly.

Skeptical: Head titled a little toward you with eyes toward you.

Sad: Lower the head and lift its arm up to its eyes. Keep your hand out of sight as much as possible.

Nervous: Vibrate the dummy's head and body, mouth open slightly.

Of course the above actions will be strengthened by the dialogue. If you have a dummy with many moving parts, many of the above actions will be different. These suggestions are to be used as guidelines to stimulate your creative imagination.

I cannot explain to you how to make your dummy laugh or cough. Every ventriloquist will do these differently. With a little patience and practice, your dummy will have his individual laugh and cough. Don't push these characteristics—they are hard on your throat at first, but with a little time and patience, you will be surprised at the variety they will add to your act.

Practice and you breathe life into your dummy. Make it so alive and real on stage and so lovable, that it will perk your audience up out of the hum-drum everyday life, and put them into another make-believe world for a few minutes. It will leave them light at heart and ready to face another day.

Chapter 10

SPEAKING FOR TWO

Buying a Script

What good would a five hundred dollar dummy be if it had nothing to say? Even a top-notch comedian would soon be out of work if he had no script.

A good script is the very essence of the act. There are a few companies where you can order scripts. But these scripts are usually designed for a particular dummy and a particular ventriloquist. Therefore, you need to revise them.

A script written for an intelligent well-mannered dummy would never be right for one that is dumb, lovable, and easy-going. In order to revise the script, you would have to change the wording throughout the script; thus losing some of the punch lines. When one dummy would answer, "yes, Ma'am," another one might answer "yep." The latter would not be able to say brilliant lines without looking out of character. For this reason, I suggest you learn how to write your own scripts.

I am not against buying scripts, but I am against using them exactly as they come. Scripts that are bought may be one of your best sources to find jokes and funny lines. Just remember to revise the scripts to fit your dummy and your situation.

If you are going to use a script that was written for someone else, read it thoroughly. If it appeals to you and will fit the personalities of both you and the dummy, you are ready to try it. But almost all scripts will need some revision. So, do the necessary revisions, like changing the "yeses" to "yeps," marking out the jokes you do not like, adding jokes you want to use, and shortening or lengthening the script to fit your time period.

The Maher Studio in Littleton, Colorado, has a wide variety of scripts on various subjects ranging from clown skits to skits prepared for use in the fight against drug abuse. They also sell joke and riddle books and jokes for use in the church.

Once a friend of mine gave me a phone number of a friend of hers. "Here," she said, "call this man and he'll write you a really good funny script for $100.00."

Well, I called. I told him all about my dummy's personality and mine on stage. I thought he was writing all this down, but I knew better when I saw the script. It wasn't made for our situation, and didn't fit the dummy's personality. Always ask for references when buying scripts from a stranger.

Later in this chapter, we will discuss how to master your script for the big moment in front of an audience.

Writing Your Own Script

If you are starting from scratch to write your own script, the basic thing you will need is jokes, gags, and riddles. Start saving them. I find that the best way to file jokes is to use a 3 X 5 file box, with the alphabet dividers.

Write each joke on a 3 X 5 index card and file for future use.

You will have to devise your own filing system. For the main topic, I put a subdivision card behind the letter. Example: Behind the "R" I would have a subdividing title "Rats" and another "Religion," plus one title "R-Misc." In the miscellaneous I would file jokes about "Rubies" or any other limited subject. It doesn't matter how you file your jokes, as long as you know how to find them.

Where do you find jokes? Everywhere. One good source is from friends and relatives. They are always happy to find jokes for you. The library is another good place. Check out several joke books at one time. By all means, get Joey Bishops' *Joke Encyclopedia*. If your library doesn't have it, ask them to borrow it for you form a school or college. Newspapers and magazines are full of jokes. Don't use them the way you find them. Sit and think about the joke, and try to make it even funnier. For example, I read this joke: "What animal is most likely to eat his relatives?" The answer is, "Aunt-eater." I used it in one of my syndicated columns like this: "Mud is so dumb; he wouldn't take his aunt to the zoo because he heard they had an anteater."

Jokes cannot be copyrighted, but always try to change a joke when you find it, and rewrite it on a card. Then you have a good feeling, like the joke is yours.

When you buy a script or joke book, and you have paid for them. Sure, they are yours to use. You can't recopy the book as is and sell it, but you can use the jokes.

The Opening Lines

Now, you have some jokes, you are ready to write a script. There are three basic parts you need to make a good script: Opening, body, and closing.

Of course, we worry about the opening first. When you first step on stage, hesitate only a second for the audience to see you and the dummy, and then go into your opening. Example: "Good evening, everyone. I am Liz LaMac, and now I would like you to meet the star of the show, Little King Joe."

The opening is longer in some routines, taking in the first few jokes. Example:

Vent: "Why were you late?"

Dummy: "I was doing my good deed for the day."

Vent: "I didn't know you did good deeds. What did you do?"

Dummy: "I helped an old lady across the street."

Vent: "Oh yeah, what took so long?"

Dummy: "She didn't want to go."

You can see that some openings take much more time. Many times in the opening you will want to use local names, especially if you are performing for a company or banquet. Example:

Vent: "Well, here we are at the local Legion Hall."

Dummy: "Who is that man with the red coat on?"

Vent: "Oh that is the president of the club, Mr. Smith. He takes care of all the activities."

Dummy: "That sounds like a good job. I hope he doesn't louse it up."

Where do you find opening lines? Watch TV. Watch and listen when a comedian is introduced. Watch the talk shows, especially at night. When a guest is introduced, there is usually an opening dialogue. Also, openings may be derived from other scripts.

The Body of the Script

The body of the routine may be many things, depending on where you are and for what kind of an audience you are playing. A few types—night clubs, schools, church school, and general.

For night clubs, the body would usually consist of a group of related mature jokes.

For general audiences, the body would consist of a group of related family-type jokes.

For schools, you need short choppy jokes. Jokes that students of all ages can understand. It is a fact that school kids love jokes about teachers, schools, principals, and animals.

The pre-school kids don't understand jokes, so the body of the routine may be a nursery rhyme or Mother Goose stories told in a funny way (include lots of actions).

For church school, the body will most likely be a Bible story. Remember to use at least one local joke at the beginning. The dummy may just mention the teacher's name or the pastor's name.

For older church groups, you may also use a Bible story or a personal testimony.

The Closing

Just before you close, it is good to mention another local name. This may be in the closing itself. Example:

Vent: "Well, Lennie, it's time for us to go."

Dummy: "Oh, I'm not going."

Vent: "What do you mean, you're not going?"

Dummy: "You see, Miss Smith is going to teach me to play the piano."

Vent: "I'll get you piano lessons when we get home."

Dummy: "No, she has to teach me. She knows all there is to know about teaching."

Vent: "Really"?

Dummy: "Yes, she is the best in the whole world."

Vent: "Who told you all this"?

Dummy;   "She did."

The closing should be brief. One of the best ways to close is with a song, as it looks very graceful and is sure to bring a good applause. If you don't sing, don't worry about it. Let the dummy sing. It doesn't even matter if the dummy isn't always in tune. There is something about a dummy singing that is entertaining. Try it. Also, watch other entertainers and comedians, to build up your file of closings.

The Thread

Now, you have a routine: opening, local joke, body, local joke, and closing. If you have all of these parts, you will have a well-balanced routine. But, if you want to add more pizzazz, more suspense, or more drama, use a running joke or what we call a "thread" throughout the whole routine.

For example, when using a nursery rhyme or Mother Goose story, the ventriloquist would be telling the story and the dummy would ask funny questions throughout. There should be a phrase or word that he repeats such as "Ah, John is that the truth?" Or "What happened next, John?"

In a running joke, the dummy starts something in the beginning, and you try to get him off the unpleasant subject. But the dummy comes back to it, bringing it up several times throughout the routine, and in the end, it should have a good punch line. Example: Dummy keeps bringing up the fact that the ventriloquist looks different, finally saying he is more different than he's been for 25 years. At the end, the dummy explodes: "I've got it. I've got it. I know why you look different. You got a new suit."

Another good touch is for the dummy to have its own by-word. It should have a little mannerism or movement of the body that happens just before the dummy says the "by-word." The audience will soon associate the two when they see the mannerism; it's like seeing the dummy thinking, and they know what's coming.

Putting It All Together

How do you get it all in your mind, so that when you are standing in front of a handful of people in your living room, or thousands in an auditorium, you can go through the routine so smoothly, that no one will notice the slightest hint of stage fright? The answer is to practice, practice, and practice.

If you are one of the rare and fortunate people who can memorize page after page of script without any trouble, you won't need to read the next paragraphs.

If You Are Forgetful

If you are one of the lucky people who have good mental recall, you may not even understand what I'm going to tell you now. You may not be able to identify with such a problem. But there are thousands (3 out of every 10) of people with dyslexia or other related differences that keep them from recalling words or thoughts exactly at the time they are needed.

And then there's the group of people who just plain "can't think straight" when it's time to speak or perform in front of an audience.

So, if for any reason you are unable to remember a whole script, this is what I suggest: Prepare props.

There's nothing wrong with it. I have dyslexia. Without props I could not have preformed one show. With props I was able to present 120 -200 shows a year. No one ever mentions my notes. I'm not even sure anyone ever noticed them.

So read your script over and over. Go over it many times in front of a mirror with your dummy. Now, pick out a key word or two in each section and joke. Fold a sheet of paper lengthwise. On one side write the key words with a marking pencil. It might go down the paper something like this:

Opening - good deed - old lady
Thread - look different
Local - good job - louse
Body – driving

I laid this folded page on one side of the stand in most cases. I have pinned notes on my dummy's back. I have never written them on my hand or sleeve but I know people who have. So, whatever works for you is fine, just don't let a little thing like dyslexia stand in your way.

Keep It Clean

Be careful when writing your scripts. Some jokes can backfire. Hostile jokes are never acceptable for any type of audience. Stay away from them. Example of a hostile joke:

Vent: How do you know when a politician is lying?

Dummy: You see his lips moving.

I used a joke in my school shows for months until I realized it wasn't a nice joke to use. It went like this:

Dummy: Who is that man?

Vent: That is Mr. _____. He is the principal of this school.

Dummy: What does he do?

Vent: He runs the school and sees that each student gets a good education.

Dummy: Does he get paid?

Vent: Yes, he takes home a pretty fat pay check.

Dummy: Sounds like a good job. I sure hope he don't get drunk and louse it up.

This joke always got a good laugh from students and teachers alike, until one day when I used it in a school assembly and it got a hesitant faked laugh. I found out later that the principal was a reformed alcoholic. There was no way I could have known this ahead of time. But I stopped using the joke. A lot of times you just have to try out new scripts and jokes and see what works and what doesn't.

There is one last thing I want to tell you concerning dialogue. Please, please, please don't ever stoop so low as to let your dummy use four-letter words. No matter what audience you are performing for, good clean jokes are better, and you will be remembered longer by more people. Oh, you might get big belly laughs at a night club when the dummy talks bad, but there will always be some people in that same audience who are offended by your bad taste and bad language. Also, a dissatisfied customer will tell more people about their dissatisfaction than will the satisfied tell about their satisfaction. In other words, the offended people are going to talk longer and louder about how bad the performer was. The ones you got the belly laughs from are just going to forget the whole thing.

Word will soon get around that you use bad language in your performance. There will be a lot of people who won't hire you because of that, so you will be losing jobs, in the long run, and losing money.

Some managers will not hire you because of the fact that they don't want you to offend a part of their audience. So try to keep your material clean. If it's good clean, wholesome fun, all types of audience are going to enjoy it. So, please remember what I say and keep your dummy's mouth clean. You will get more work and much, much more respect. And remember if there are children present they will take in every word you say. And you become the teacher. Don't lead them astray.

Chapter 11

DIALOGUE, JOKES AND SCRIPTS

A Script from Hee Haw's Archie Campbell

I know one thing about Archie Campbell, the entertainer from the long running TV show "Hee Haw": he never had dyslexia. One day we were talking and I said, "I would sure like to have a good script for Charlie Bird."

Archie said, "Give me a piece of paper, I'll write you an old script that I used to use years ago." Well, he wrote the following script without even stopping to think twice. I suppose it's as old as the hills. But it's still good and funny and Archie knew it word for word.

But first let me tell you this amusing story about Archie. It happened about two months after he wrote the script for Charlie Bird. I was back stage at the Grand Ole Opry in Nashville, chatting with some friends in the lounge. And I happened to look over at the monitor and realized that Archie Campbell was performing at that moment on the stage. I hurried out to the stage and was amazed to hear Archie and one of his sons "doing the act" that he had written down for me. They did a wonderful job and the audience loved it.

After they came off stage I asked Archie, "Wasn't that the script you wrote for me and Charlie Bird?"

"Sure was," said Archie. "Writing it down for you made me remember what a good script it was. I've used it several times since. But you can still use it; no one ever remembers a script."

The Script from Archie Campbell

C: Hey Liz, these hunters are scaring me to death, I need some insurance.

L: Well, you're in luck, I'm an insurance agent.

C: How much does it cost?

L: Ten cents per day.

C: That's reasonable, what are the benefits?

L: Well if you lose an arm or leg, we'll help you hunt it.

C: (Charlie bird does a double take.)

L: Seriously, I can insure you, but first I'll have to fill out your form—name?

C: James.

L: That your first name?

C: Yes.

L: Your last name?

C: James.

L: That your first name?

C: That's right.

L: You mean your name is James James?

C: No, my name is James J. James.

L: What does the J. stand for?

C: James.

L: Born?

C: Of course.

L: I know that—where were you born?

C: Upstairs—in a nest.

L: When?

C: Early one morning (laugh) 7:00.

L: How do you know it was 7:00?

C: I had the alarm set.

L: How many in the family?

C: Lets see—14.

L: Golly, 14 altogether?

C: No, just one at a time.

C: Every one of them were boys.

L: All boys, oh?

C: Yeah, except the girls, and they all had the same name.

L: Really?

C: Yep—all the boys were named Jack, except Bill, his name was Joe.

L: How about your nationality?

C: I'm a Republican.

L: No, that's your politics, by that I mean wherever you were born, that's what you are.

C: You're kidding?

L: No, if you were born in Germany, you're a German. Born in France, you're a Frenchman. Born in Poland, you're a Pole.

C: Repeat that last line.

L: If you were born in Poland, you're a Pole.

C: Then, if I was born in Holland, would I be a Hole?

L: Ok—how about your occupation?

C: I'm a Baptist.

L: No, that's your belief.

C: No, that's my occupation.

L: You don't understand, now. I'll show you the difference—I'm a young, beautiful, hard working, successful entertainer.

C: What's that?

L: That is my occupation.

C: No, that is your belief.

L: How about your parents?

C: Yeah, how about them.

L: What are their names?

C: Pop and Mom.

L: Give me their names?

C: James.

L: Now don't tell me your daddy's name is James J. James?

C: No, his name is James O. James.

L: What does the O. stand for?

C: Opium.

L: But opium is a dope.

C: Oh, do you know my dad?

Jokes from Speck Rhodes

The following is one of the jokes Speck Rhodes, from the Porter Wagoner TV show, gave me for Charlie Bird:

Speck: Charlie Bird how do you like my suit?

C.B.:   Oh, it's ok but ain't it awful loud, Speck?

Speck: Yes, but I like checked suits.

C.B.:   What kind of suit is it?

Speck: It's a Sear Sucker suit.

C.B.:   Sear Sucker?

Speck: Yes, Sears sold it and I was a sucker to buy it.

Mud and Dud

*Mud and Dud are two seemingly innocent plaques that hang on the palace wall in Liz's TV series "King Joe's Palace." Liz works them from behind the wall. A small monitor helps her see what is going onto the tape.

In my first column, "Frogs and Spices," I had jokes with Mud and Dud. Later when we filmed the TV series I wanted to use the old Mud and Dud jokes. And after much searching I found bodies for them. They were made from a pair of comedy house shoes. And that is how Mud and Dud became the King's ancestors. And then I used their modified old jokes for the new Mud and Dud of the TV series and the new newspaper column, "Dummyland Panorama." I used two other voices with Mud and Dud.

This is a good example for what Irby Mandrell taught me: Use where you are as stepping stones. Don't be starting over all the time. Stay in the same grove and use your past experiences as stepping stones.

And that's just what I did with Mud and Dud's characters; they were just names I had used in my children's column. But many people had read that column and remembered Mud and Dud. And when I found their bodies and used them as Uncle Mud and his brother Dud, these people were happy to see them at last. So, don't be starting over all the time. Always use where you are as stepping stones. And as Irby also says, you can always upgrade later.

CHAPTER 12

DISTANT VOICE TECHNIQUES

To Obtain a Distant Voice

To obtain a distant voice, you take a deep breath, and as you speak, think about the vocal cords. Think they are tight and they are squeezing the air as it is being pushed through them by the stomach muscles. There is nothing difficult about obtaining the distant voice, but it is hard on your throat until you have built up the proper muscles. These muscles in the throat are slow to respond. So, take your time and be patient. Practice only a few minutes at a time, and not more than three times a day. If your throat hurts, the best thing to do is stop. If you get hoarse, don't try it again for several days. But just keep at it until you are satisfied that the voice sounds distant enough. You can hold your hand lightly on your throat and feel the vibrations of the distant voice.

Roof and Cellar Voice

There are different aspects of the distant voice. First, we will learn the voice that is above us, the roof voice. To do the roof voice, think the air coming through the vocal cords up against the roof of the mouth.

For the down in the cellar voice, you will think the air down the throat. "Thinking the air in your stomach" might be a better way to put it.

As I sat here trying to better describe the way to obtain the roof and cellar voice, I came to the following conclusions:

1. When I'm saying, "hello down there," trying to make the words sound as if they are above me, I pitched my voice higher on the scale.

2. When I tried to say in the cellar voice, "what you doing up there," I pitched my voice much lower on the scale.

3. There was very little voice projection through the mouth. The sound was not being forced out of my mouth onto the cold mirror.

4. The sound was being forced up the back of my throat for the roof voice and down the throat for the cellar voice.

I then took a mirror and held it close to my lips. I said in my normal voice, "Hello down there." And the mirror steamed over because of the warm air from my breath being forced out of my mouth onto the mirror.

I then held the mirror close to my lips and said, "Hello down there" in the ventriloquial roof voice. No steam appeared on the glass. Because there was no air forced through my mouth. The sound was being forced with the help of my tongue, up the back of my throat, thus producing a distant sound. And because I was saying, "hello down there" and directing my attention and others' attention upward, the voice was coming from above us;

we all heard it from above. Again, this is what I did and now you try it.

1. For the roof voice pitch the voice higher on the scale.

2. For the cellar voice, pitch the voice lower on the scale.

3. Hold a mirror close to your lips. Say, "Hello down there" in your normal voice. Notice the steam on the mirror.

4. Hold the mirror close to your lips and say, "Hello down there," while pitching your voice higher on the scale: while thinking the voice up in the back of your throat and while squeezing the vocal cords together to make the voice sound distant. If there is little or no moisture on the mirror; you may be on the right track to finding the distant voice.

5. Repeat the same procedure for cellar voice. Only this time think down in the throat, and pitch the voice lower on the scale.

Only practice this for a few minutes at a time. It could give you a headache. Rest often and drink warm drinks. Hot water with lemon juice and a clove is very good.

Distant Voice Exercises

We are going to use the knowledge we already have learned concerning the distant sounds. We are going to practice the ventriloquial "roof voice," "cellar voice," "plain distant voice," and "near ventriloquial voice."

We will begin with the vowels A-E-I-O-U. Using the letter "A" say it 5 times once in a normal voice: once in the "roof voice," next in the "cellar voice," in the plain distant voice, and in near ventriloquial voice. It will make steam on the mirror but not as much as your normal voice. It may well be the near ventriloquial voice you use for your dummy. It is called near ventriloquial voice. It isn't above or below you. But when you practice like this it will sound a little distant from you, and that is what you need for your dummy. He needs to sound a little distance away from you.

Here we go:

"A" normal

"A" roof voice

"A" cellar voice

"A" plain distant voice, neither up nor down, but back in your throat.

"A" near ventriloquial voice

To help; physically add these actions—as you say "A" in the roof voice, raise your hands in the air (palm sides up) as if to actually push the voice up. Do this hand movement in an exaggerated fashion.

Push the hands (palm side down) as you do the "A" in the cellar voice. Push hands back (palms leading) as you do the plain distant voice, and push palms back as you project the "A" out in the near ventriloquial voice. But not with the same force, because it doesn't need to sound that far away.

Here we go again, say:

"A" in our normal voice, projecting the air out in front of us and opening the mouth wide in exaggerated fashion.

"A" while pushing the air up with the palms of the hand, at the same time we are thinking "up in the back of the throat," and keeping the lips still.

"A" while pushing the air down with the palms of our hands, while thinking "down in the throat" and keeping the lips still.

"A" while pushing the air back behind us while thinking "back in the throat and out the back of the neck," and far away, keeping the lips still.

"A" while pushing the air back behind us while thinking, "near ventriloquial voice." Still not using the normal voice but trying to achieve a near distant sound keeping the lips still.

Don't be discouraged if at first the sounds or voices are very similar. They will progress and become distant as we practice, and practice and practice.

After you have practiced each of the vowels in the above fashion, substitute the word "Hello" for the vowels. Next, try the "baa" of a sheep. If you do this right and repeat it over and over, it will sound like a lot of sheep. Alternate from near distant to far distant.

The Telephone Voice

After you have mastered the distant voice, the telephone voice will not be difficult to master. It is achieved in the same way, only you think about the vocal cords being squeezed in the center. Try until you get a metallic voice that sounds like a person over the phone. It just takes practice until you are satisfied; using a real phone when you practice will help tremendously. Pick up the receiver and say "Hello." Answer in a metallic like distant voice, "Hello." Keep trying and it will soon come out right.

You can add a few minutes to your act by letting a phone ring. Of course it is someone calling the dummy. You can work up a little routine about the maid having trouble at home, or it might be the baby, or dog sitter having an emergency. Maybe the dog is sick: "from eating your cooking." But whatever you do make the call brief. Novelties are for variety and are great if they are short and leave the people wondering how you did that, and wanting more.

You can order a life-like phone that uses batteries. You ring it anytime you want by pushing a button that you have hidden in your pocket or in the dummy's back you might find one at a magic shop.

Voice in the Bottle

First of all, when you stand in front of a crowd and inform them that a little man is trapped in the bottle, and that you are going to talk to him, they expect to hear him talk back to you and they expect the voice to come from the bottle.

So they are expecting to hear a voice from the bottle. You're halfway home, now. They are expecting a distant voice. So, if you do a half way decent job they will love it.

And when you are holding a bottle in your hand, and talking to a person in it, it will help you to try harder to get that voice to sound as if it is coming from the bottle. Here again, illusion is playing a big part in obtaining the result. You say, "He's in the bottle." You look in the bottle, you ask him a question, and everyone expects him to answer from within the bottle. And as you tip the bottle slightly, your lips are still, yet a voice says, "Let me out of here," we all hear the man in the bottle speak. The illusion is complete.

The voice in the bottle should be in between the near ventriloquistic voice and the distant voice. The size of the bottle and the distance you are holding it from your body, will also play a part here. Just play around with it and practice different sounds until you are satisfied with the voice.

Muffled Voice

The muffled voice is made by pressing the end of the tongue to the floor of the mouth. This lumps the tongue back in the mouth. While in this position, push plenty of air up from your diaphragm using stomach muscles and say, "Let me out!"

The tongue position will lessen the sibilants (s, t, f), and the words will come out muffled.

Illusion plays an important part here. If you see a ventriloquist hold his hand over the dummy's mouth and the dummy is squirming and trying to talk, you want— and will hear—the words come out muffled.

It is very effective to hold your hand over the dummy's mouth and let him say a few words in the muffled voice, and then remove your hand letting the rest of the sentence come out in his regular voice. Practice this. It's fun.

There is one thing to remember when you are using a distant voice: whether it be a phone voice or a man in a bottle, identify the person who is going to talk. Before the audience hears the voice, they should, in most cases, know who is doing the talking. So, give your character a name, a personality, and your audience will hear him more distinctly.

The Baby Cry

A few years ago I received a post card from Col. Bill Boley. He said, "I am looking forward to seeing you

103

at the Vent Convention in June and am anxious to hear your new 'baby cry.'"

Well, my daughter picked up the card and read it and asked, "What kind of weird people do you hang with Mom? He wants to hear your baby cry."

Well, that does sound "off the wall" but Col. Bill Boley has one of the best "baby cry voices" I've ever heard. Bill is a large man, and when he holds that little baby and it cries, it's very amusing and effective. He once used a baby in his school act. He pushed a buggy on stage telling the kids that his wife was sick, and he had to bring the baby along. But, he hoped it would sleep through the show. Sure enough, about half way through the show, the baby awoke, screaming its lungs out. Col. Bill asked if anyone in the audience had babies at home. Hands went up all over the room. Then, Col. Boley asked for a volunteer to help him. A boy came running up on stage. And just as the Col. was putting the blanket bundled baby in the boy's arms, it wet all over the boys hands. Everyone screamed with laughter. Most kids had baby brothers and sisters at home and weren't bothered by the water. They were used to it.

And of course, Col. Bill explained to me that he had a little ear syringe filled with water under the blanket and could squeeze it anytime he chose to and in any direction he wanted the stream of water to flow. Col. Bill has worked for several years on the cruise ships of Carnival Cruise Lines. He's a fine ventriloquist and loves to share and help others.

For the baby cry, lump the tongue back in the mouth and try to imitate the crying of a baby. It is also between a near and distant ventriloquistic voice with maybe a little muffled sound.

The baby cry is very effective when it is mastered and used in a good script. After reading the chapter on dialogue, you will be able to write scripts using the "baby cry." It is very difficult to teach one to imitate the baby cry. Just keep trying. Practice and you'll get it, by trial and error if nothing else.

I want to emphasize to <u>never try to throw the voice over the audience.</u> You may use a distant voice in front of them, to the side, or behind you, but <u>never, never behind them.</u>

By now you realize it is very difficult to write instructions for the distant voice. I didn't master a really good distant voice until I went to the ventriloquist convention, and I actually saw and heard it being demonstrated. Then I found an old pamphlet, written in the 1800s, on the subject. With what I had seen and heard at the convention, and what I read in the pamphlet, I finally got it together. These are the same instructions that I have given you. Once I decided I wanted to get a distant voice, I never stopped practicing until I found it. So, what I am trying to tell you is to just keep practicing and trying, and soon you will find a distant voice. It is more trial and error than anything else. Again it all comes with practice, practice and practice and some more practice.

The Voice across the Stage Bit

This bit didn't actually require a distant voice, but it appeared that I was throwing my voice across the stage. It was truly an illusion. It was very effective, and the audience loved it. And it was fun practicing and presenting it on stage. I always enjoy working on stage. I never take my act too seriously. If I make a mistake I laugh about it and go on.

In this bit, my dummy Little Joe is sitting on my knee. Little Joe wants to sing Rocky Top. I say, no, one of the band members has already or is going to sing Rocky Top.

But Little Joe insists, saying he is rich and can do anything he wants. He calls out to one of the Sugar Daddies (band members), and Michael Robinson comes running over to us. Little Joe whispers in his ear and Michael jumps back saying, "How much?" Again Little Joe whispers in his ear. This time we all hear him say, "Five hundred dollars."

Michael says, "You got a deal, Little Joe," and he takes Little Joe to the other side of the stage, and he and Joe talk and sing Rocky Top. This took a lot of practice. Every word had to be said exactly as practiced and to make sure it was, the script was taped on the chair on the other side of the stage. It was taped by Michael's foot and on my chair where my foot was. That way it was easier for me to talk for the dummy while he was across stage on Michael's knee. Again, I didn't use the distant voice, but the illusion was that I "threw my voice" across stage.

POSTSCRIPT

WE DELIVER SMILES

My husband and I shared the same goal in life. Our goal was to DELIVER SMILES. Now, through these smiles, I want to be instrumental in the healing process. I want to help make the world a better place to live through laughter.

When I am on the stage I sometimes look out over the audience and see people who are hurting and sad. Some are mental patients; others are just people with problems and worries. When I see the sad and distressed look on their faces, I say a little prayer, "Dear God, help me break their worry cycle, for just a few minutes, by bringing them into my world of fantasy."

There is a story behind this "worry cycle." I don't know where I got the term, but I have used it for years. My mother was a first-class worrier. In other words, my mother was a worry wart. Many times, she worried herself sick. I was a very small child when my brother was called into the Army. My mother worried about him all the time. Sometimes she would go to his closet and stand with her arms around his clothes, and cry. I was always afraid that she would go out of her mind with worry, or that she would die of worry, if he didn't come home soon.

I found out at an early age, that if I could make my mother laugh and get her involved in something light, like singing old songs, old hymns, or telling old stories, she would stop worrying.

The worrying soon started back again, and the worried look would come back on her face, but not with the same force. It seemed to build up with time.

As I got older I thought of this as a worry cycle. I figured if I could stop my mother's worry cycle long enough for her to feel better, then I could stop the worry cycle for others. You know, it has worked.

I can look out on the audience, and watch the smiles spread across the tense faces and know that the worry cycle is being broken. I can see the people get caught up in the fascination of the dummy, and I can see them leaving their worries behind for a brief time. I know I have broken their worry cycle. I can almost feel the healing power at work, and when they leave the auditorium, their faces are a little softer than when they came in. Sometimes, there are still smiles on their faces as they go to their cars. This gives me a good feeling.

Being a ventriloquist has been good for me. I sincerely pray that you will receive some of the joys and satisfactions that I have known.

GLOSSARY

VENTRILOQUIAL (adj.) Ven-tri-lo-qui-al: Having to do with, practicing, or resembling ventriloquism. Example: The man spoke in his ventriloquial voice.

VENTRILOQUIAL DUMMY: A dummy or doll used by a ventriloquist. It may also be called a dummy, figure, vent figure, vent doll or puppet. I prefer to call it a dummy. Dummy is a fun word and is catching. But remember, don't confuse "dummy" with "dumb."

VENTRILOQUIALLY (adv.) Ven-tri-lo-qui-al-ly: Pertaining to ventriloquism. Example: The man was speaking, ventriloquially, through his dummy.

VENTRILOQUISM (noun) Ven-tril-o-quism: The art of speaking or producing more than one voice or sound and making that voice or sound appear to come from an object or person other than the speaker. Example: The girl was practicing ventriloquism through her dummy.

VENTRILOQUIST (noun) Ven-tril-o-quist: A person who practices ventriloquism. Example: The ventriloquist and his dummy are ready to perform.

VENTRILOQUISTIC (adj.) Ven-tril-o-quis-tic: Of ventriloquial nature. Example: The pencil is sometimes used as a ventriloquistic aid.

VENTRILOQUIZE (verb) Ven-tril-o-quize: To speak or utter as a ventriloquist. Example: She was asked to ventriloquize for the party.

VENTRILOQUOUS (adj.) Ven-tril-o-quous: Resembling or having to do with ventriloquism. Example: With a puppet on her hand, she spoke in a ventriloquous fashion.

VENTRILOCUTION (noun) Ven-tri-lo-cu-tion: Pertaining to the voice used by the ventriloquist for the dummy or puppet. Example: His ventrilocution showed that he had a wide voice range.

VENTRILOQUY (noun) Ven-tril-o-quy: Same as ventriloquism. Example: This book is about ventriloquy.

19.97

Made in the USA
Monee, IL
27 February 2021